# HAVING FAITH THROUGH GOD'S WORD ON YOUR LIFE'S JOURNEY

Barbara Brown

ISBN: 0692685340
ISBN 13: 9780692685341

*Dedicated to my three sons*
*Calvin Brown, my adopted son Darryl Brown*
*and my beloved son Stanley Brown.*

# INTRODUCTION

This book will share my personal experiences of being a God fearing Christian. I wrote this book to understand who is a true Christian according to God's word. I began to question myself and others on why some Christians showed a dark side that what was not how the Bible states how they should live. I wanted to read what the Bible say's and are we living up to treating each other the way we should. Some Christians turn their backs on people whether they be a Christian or not. Some of us all have gone astray, and were not following God's word. This can be since we may not have read how we should live as a Christian during our life's journey. Not knowing may cause some of us to depend on our own choices. If we make poor choices they could affect us the rest of our lives and how we treat each other.

During this time a struggling Christian need love and support on their journey. Reaching out to them in their most vulnerable stage. The following scriptures will be quoted directly from the Bible on how God stated we should live. If we live according to the word this will allow us to enter into his kingdom. If we choose not to, then we have to pay the price of our souls not being excepted in eternal life. According to the Bible I have tried to live my life, by following his word. Even though I am still learning I want to leave this world and know I have done my best. My gift from God is to write the understanding I have come into as I grow. We are not here to live forever, because one day we all will answer a higher power.

Life has many journeys and can be unpredictable starting from birth through adulthood. Through all these cycles we grow from all the people who are placed in our lives. Some of our experiences can be good or bad. We all encounter different cycles during our whole life. We all make choices depending on what we think are best for us. Even before we were born our parents already set the stage before us. We cannot choose who our parents are and where we will live. Even their economic status will determine whether we will be born poor or rich. It is up to each one of us to decide as we grow into adult to listen to our inner spirit guiding us in all the stages of our lives. It is important to be a good role model for ourselves and others.

According to the word of God there are many fallen Christians. They live their lives, by pretending they are true Christian not following God's word. They go about deceiving those that come in their path. I was raised in church at a very early age. During my life cycle I went from church to church looking for those perfect Christians living, by God's word. I became very disappointed to find some Christians were not living up to God's word. Being raised in foster care and living on my own as a teenager, I became pregnant at a very early age. My foster mom was a good Christian, so I am thankful for being raised in a good solid Christian home. I was encouraged to read the Bible and newspaper at a very early. My foster mom and dad were very involved in the Baptist Church. My foster dad was an usher and my foster mom was a nurse. They stayed married more than fifty years. They both showed each other a lot of respect and love, he called her baby and treated her like a lady. He was a real gentleman. He loved all of the foster children and never had an unkind word to say. I am glad to be able to experience the life on what a true Christian family life is. This has stayed with me all my life, as I am growing and learning what God's word says. What is a true Christian? And how will you know? Their lives should speak for how they follow God's word.

You have to ask yourself during your life's journey what are the most important decisions you should make? Those decisions will influence every aspect of your life. They will also make a difference to everyone that walks in your path. Rather you decide to make good or bad choices will determine your life from the beginning to the end. We cannot expect the poor choices that we make may cause others to go astray. They can follow in our footsteps without the knowledge of right and wrong.

God's choices will guide us to become successful and have a less painful journey. Allowing us in the end we will receive our reward from the most highest power. In our life this is why we have to constantly question our ??? On all we do in life. Whether we are causing others to go in the wrong direction or right direction. We then will be held accountable for the sins they fall into. Making poor decisions such as being lustful, not honoring God's word with no respect, lying causing others to not be responsible from their wrongs. Sleeping with different partners bringing children into the world who wound up with no direction. This leads to poverty causing crime in many of the neighborhoods that lead to fear, of not knowing if you can become a victim.

There are some people who hide their identity of who they really are. They can lure people who are spinned in their spider web. They have no empathy or compassion for others. These personalities can come from anyone from the young to old. A person's life can be taken at any given moments. Not being aware of how to protect themselves they can become a prey. This is why on our journey we have to live life with guidance of the Holy Spirit that we can't see, but living day to day being guided by the spirit is a way to protect us from harm and danger. The human instinct is able to comprehend. As the scripture states "For we should walk in faith and not by sight for we wrestle against principalities in high places. The flesh is weak, but the spirit is strong." Our lives should not be based on the predictions of people. This can cause one to become deceived in a life of despair, by being in the wrong situation. We have to live day to day setting ourselves up to be in control by allowing the Holy Spirit to be our guide, or our life's journey. We can learn to appreciate how the Holy Spirit brought us through situation; we would not have been able to overcome on our own.

When the time comes for us to have an understanding of life. This is when we are faced with what direction we should take. These decisions will predict our choices on our life long journey for good or bad. If we accept the good life it can be in our best interest. Even through our struggles of ups and downs we can live a positive life. This allows us to become victimizers. The down side of making the wrong decisions and over stepping over certain boundaries can cause our journey to have a devastating affect for the rest of our lives.

Anyone who becomes a part of our lives will also suffer from the consequences. This is the reason as some people would say bad luck or curses passed on throughout each generation. Now we have to get the stage for others to follow. Being trapped in a web of the sins of life. These sins will dictate your life on how you handle different situations you are faced with. There is no escaped unless one turn to a higher power to give them the strength to overcome. These decisions can cause one's life to become short lived, because their life has no substance to sustain them through the pitfalls they face. They fall into darkness assuming another identity of who they really are. It's like wearing different masks, so others will not know who you really are. There is a scripture in the Bible that states "Lord teach me the things that I cannot change and to know the difference." Even though a person do all they can to become productive to society there are others where you can become a prey in their evil ways. As the Bible share "The devil goes around like a roaring lion seeking, those he may devour". Life and destiny begins from our beginning and end of our journey. Our final moment will depend on how we lived our life.

As the Bible quoted in Psalm 95:1 - "O come let us sing unto the Lord: let us make a joyful noise to the rock of our salvation. Let us come before his presence with thanksgiving and make a joyful noise unto him with psalms. For the Lord is a great God and a great king above all Gods. In his hands are the deep places of the earth the strength of the hills is his also. The sea is his, and he made it and his hands formed the dry land. O come let us worship and bow down let us kneel before the Lord our maker. For he is our God and we are the people of his pasture and the sheep of his hand. Today if ye will hear his voice. Harden not your heart as in the provocation and as in the day of temptation in the wilderness. When your fathers tempted me proved me and saw my works. Forty years long was I grieved with this generation and said, it is a people that do err in their heart, and they have not known my ways. Unto whom I share my wrath that they should not enter into my rest. O sing unto the Lord a new song sing unto the Lord in all the earth. Declare his glory among the heathen his wonders among all people. For the Lord is great and greatly to be praised he is to be feared above all Gods. For all the Gods of the nations are idols but the Lord made the heavens. Honor and majesty are before him strength and beauty is in his sanctuary. Give unto the Lord O ye kindred's of the people give unto the lord glory and strength. O worship the Lord in the beauty of holiness fear before him all the earth. Say among the heathen that the Lord reigneth the world also shall be established that it shall not be moved he shall judge the people righteously. Before the Lord for he cometh for he cometh to judge the earth he shall judge the world with righteousness and the people with truth. Ye that love the Lord hate evil he preserveth the soul of his saints he deliver them out the hand of the wicked. Light is ??? For the righteous and gladness for the upright in heart."

Wherefore as the Holy Ghost Saith, Today if ye will hear his voice. Harden not your hearts, as in the provocation in the day of temptation in the wilderness. When your father's tempted me, proved me and saw my works for forty years. Wherefore I was grieved with that generation and said they do always err in their heart and they have not known my ways. So I swore in my wrath they shall not enter into my rest. Take heed brethren lest there be in any of you an evil heart of unbelief, in departing from the living God. But exort one another daily while it is glad today lest any of you be hardened through the deceitfulness of sin. For we are made partakers of Christ, if we hold the beginning of our confidence steadfast unto the end. While it is said to day if ye will his voice harden not your hearts as in the provocation." "But when ye pray use not vain repetitions as the heathen do for they think that they shall be heard for their much speaking.

Be not ye therefore like unto them for your father knoweth what things ye have need of, before ye ask him. After this manner therefore pray ye Our Father which art in heaven, Hallowed be thy name. Thy kingdom come, thy will be done in earth, as it is in heaven Give us this day our daily bread. And forgive us our debts, as we forgive our debtors. And lead us not into temptation but deliver us from evil, for thine is the kingdom, and the power, and the glory forever. Amen." For if ye forgive men their trespasses your heavenly Father will also forgive you. But if ye forgive not men their trespasses, neither will your Father forgive your trespasses.

Lay not up yourselves treasures upon earth, where moth and rust doth corrupt, and where thieves break through and steal. But lay up for yourselves treasures in heaven, where neither moth now rust doth corrupt and where thieves do not break through nor steal. But lay up for yourselves treasures in heaven, where neither moth now rust doth corrupt and where thieves do not break through nor steal. For where your treasure is, there will your heart be also the light of the body is the eye if therefore thine eye be single, thy whole body shall be full of light. But if thine eye be evil thy whole body shall be full of darkness. If therefore the light that is in thee be darkness how great is that darkness. No man can serve two masters for either he will hate the one and love the other or else he will hold to the one and despise the other. Ye cannot serve God and mammon. Therefore I say unto you take no thought for your life what he shall eat or what ye shall drink not yet for your body what ye shall put on. Is not the life more than meat and the body than raiment.

Behold the fowls of the air for they sow not, neither do they reap, nor gather into barns, yet your heavenly Father feedeth them; Are ye not much better than they? Consider the lilies of the field, how they grow they toil not, neither do they spin. Wherefore if God so clothe the grass of the field, which today is and tomorrow is cast into the oven, shall be not much more clothe you oye of little faith. But seek ye first the kingdom of God and his righteousness and all these things shall be added unto you. Take therefore no thought for the morrow for the morrow shall take thought for the things of itself." "Give not that which is holy unto the dogs, neither cast ye your pearls before swine lest they trample them under their feet and turn again and rend you. Ask and it shall be given you seek and ye shall find knock and it shall be opened unto you. For everyone that asketh receiveth and he that seeketh findeth and to him that knocketh it shall be opened. If ye then being evil know how to give good gifts unto your children how much more shall your Father which is in heaven give good things to them that ask him. Enter ye in at the strait gate for wide is the gate and broad is the way which leadeth to destruction and many there be which go in their thereat. Because strait is the gate and narrow in the way, which leadeth unto life, and few there be that find it. Beware of false prophets which come to you in sheep's clothing, but inwardly they are ravening wolves. Ye shall know them by their fruits. Do men gather grapes of thorns or figs of thistles. Even so every good tree bringeth forth good fruit, but a corrupt three bringeth forth evil fruit. Every three that bringeth not forth good fruit is hewn down and cast into the fire. Wherefore by their fruits ye shall know them. Not everyone that saith unto me, Lord! Lord! shall enter into the kingdom of heaven but he that doeth the will of my Father which is in heaven. Many will say to me in that day Lord, Lord, have we not prophesied in thy name? and in thy name have cast out clouds? And in thy name done many wonderful works? And then will I profess unto them I never knew you depart from me ye that work iniquity.

Therefore whosoever hearth these sayings of mine, and cloth them I will liken him unto a wise man, which built his house upon a rock. And the rain descended and the floods came, and the winds blew, and beat upon that house and it fell not for it was founded upon a rock. And everyone that heaveth these sayings of mine and doth them not, shall be likened unto a foolish man, which built his house upon the sand. And the rain descended and the floods came, and the winds blew and beat upon that house, and it fell and great was the fall of it."

As Jesus quoted in his word how we should concentrate on doing positive things in our lives. This will keep us strong through difficult times. Throughout our lives we will all face challenges. Some of them can be very difficult to face, but as long as we stay strong in God he promises to bring us through as long as we put our trust in him. Through any adversary's we can remain strong in the hope of being created with our Father in heaven knowing it was him who brought us through. If we allow ourselves to fall into the deadly sins of life we can only have ourselves to blame for not obeying his word. The people who we followed and lead us astray. They will not be there to our rescue, by settles traps for us to fall into. A "we have to ??? Father which is in heaven forgives us our sins for we also forgive everyone that indebted to us. And lead us not into temptation but deliver us from evil." Why should we have to experience a life of sin long negative experiences? Do not be fooled by all that glitters is not gold. Some of us remain gullible and have by not knowing the best path to follow. This can come from not having positive role models in our lives. It makes it easy for people who are in the same situations to spot those that can be vulnerable.

It usually can be the opposite sex the majority of the time. Even people of the same sex can expose us all types of sins. They destroy others lives by causing their life to be a life of hell leading them to a early death to face. From their life coming to a end. They do not have the time to ask for forgiveness, it is too late to make a change. This change can only come while we are still alive on earth. We have to live a life that is pleasing to our Father which is in heaven. He wants us all to live a healthy and prosperous life, by growing in wisdom and knowledge of his word. Then we are able to show others the blessing

God has bestowed on us. "Or hath God assayed to go and take him a nation from the midst of another nation by temptations, by signs and by wonders, and by war, and by a mighty hand, and by a stretched out arm, and by great terrors, according to all that the Lord your God did for you in Egypt before your eyes? Unto thee it was shewed that thou misest know that the Lord he is God there is none else beside him. Thou shalt keep therefore his statutes, and his commandments, which I command thee this day, that it may go well with thee, and that thou may go well with thee, and that thou mayest prolong thy days upon the earth, which the Lord thy God giveth thee forever." "The great temptations which thine eyes saw, and the signs, and the wonders, and the mighty hand, and the stretched out arm, whereby the Lord thy God brought thee out so shall the Lord thy God do unto all the people of whom thou are afraid. The great temptations which thine have seen, the signs, and those great miracles." "Be strong and of a good courage, fear not, nor be afraid of them for the Lord thy God he it is that doth go with thee he will not fail thee nor forsake thee" "Serving the Lord with all humility of mind, and with the many tears, and temptations which befell me by the lying in wait of the Jews." "Now the God of peace that brought again from the dead our Lord Jesus, that great shepherd of the sheep through the blood of the everlasting covenant. Make you perfect in every good work to do his will, working in you that which is well pleasing in his sight, through Jesus Christ to whom be glory forever and ever Amen."

Who are kept by the power of God through faith unto salvation ready to be revealed in the last time. Wherein ye greatly rejoice, though now a season, if need be, ye are in heaviness through manifold temptations. That the trial of your faith being much more precious than of gold that perisheth though it be tried with fire might be found unto praise and honor and glory at the appearing of Jesus Christ. Receiving the end of your faith even the salvation of your souls. Unto whom it was revealed that not unto themselves, but unto us they did minister the things which are now reported unto you by them that have preached the gospel unto you with the Holy Ghost sent down from heaven which things the angels desire to look into. Wherefore gird up the loins of your mind, be sober and hope to the end for the grace that is to be brought unto you at the revelation of Jesus Christ. As obedient children not fashioning yourselves according to the former lust in your ignorance. But as he which hath called you is holy, so be ye holy in all manner of conversation. Because it is written, be ye holy for I am holy."

"But there were false prophets also among the people, even as there shall be false teachers among you, who privily shall bring in damnable heresies even denying the Lord that brought them, and bring upon themselves swift destruction. And many shall follow their pernicious ways, by reason of whom the way of truth shall evil be spoken of. And through covetousness shall they with feigned words make merchandise of you whose judgment now of a long time lingereth not and their damnation slumbereth not. For if God spared not the angels that sinned, but cast them down to hell and delivered them into chains of darkness, to be reserved unto judgment. The Lord knoweth how to deliver the Godly out of temptation and to reserve the unjust unto the day of judgment to be punished.

But chiefly them that walk after the flesh in the lust of uncleanness and despise government. Presumptuous are they self willed, they are not afraid to speak evil of dignities. Whereas angels which are greater in power and might, bring not railing accusation against them before the Lord. But these, as natural brute beasts, made to be taken and destroyed, speak evil of the thing they understand not, and shall utterly perish in their own corruption. And shall receive the reward of unrighteousness, as they that count it pleasure to riot in the day time. Spots they are and blemishes sporting themselves with their own deceivings while they feast with you. Having eyes full of adultery and that cannot cease from sin beguiling unstable souls and heart they have exercised with covetous practices cursed children, which have forsaken the right way and are gone astray following the way of Salaam the son of Bosor, who loved the wage of unrighteousness. For when they speak great swelling words of vanity, they allure through the lusts of the flesh, through much wantonness, those that were clean escaped from them who live in error. While they promise them liberty, they themselves are the servant of corruption for of whom a man is overcome of the same is he brought in bondage. For if after they have escaped the pollutions of the world through knowledge of the Lord and Savior Jesus Christ they are again entangled therein and overcome the latter end is worse with them than the beginning. For it had been better for them not to have known the way of righteousness than after they have known it to turn from the holy commandment delivered unto them. But it is happened unto them according to the true proverb, the dog is turned to his own vomit again and the son that was washed to her wallowing in the mire. Knowing this first that there shall come in the last days scoffers walking after them own lusts. And saying where is the promise of his coming? For since the fathers fell asleep all things continue as they were from the beginning of the creation. For this they willingly are ignorant of, that by the word of God the heavens were of old and the earth standing out of the water and in the water. Whereby the world that then was being overflowed with water perished. But the heavens and the earth, which are now, by the same word are kept in store reserved unto fire against the day of judgment and perdition of ungodly men. But beloved be not ignorant of this one thing, that one day is with the Lord as a thousand years and a thousand years as one day. The Lord is not slack concerning his promise, as some men count slackness, but is long suffering to us-ward not willing that any should perish but that all should come to repentance. But the day of the Lord will come as a thief in the night in the which the heavens shall pass away with a great noise, and the elements shall melt with fervent heat, the earth also and the works that are therein shall be burned up to. Seeing then that all these things shall be dissolved what manner of persons ought ye to be in all holy conversation and godliness. Looking for and hasting unto the coming of the day of God wherein the heavens being on fire shall be dissolved, and the elements shall melt with fervent heat. Nevertheless we according to his promise, look for new heaven and

new earth, where in dwelleth righteousness. Wherefore, beloved, seeing that ye look for such things, be diligent that ye may be found of
him in peace, without spot, and blameless. And account that the long
suffering of our Lord is salvation even as our beloved brother Paul
also according to the wisdom given unto him hath written unto you.
As also in all his epistles speaking in them of these things in which
are some things hard to be understand which are unlearned and
unstable wrest, as they do also the other scriptures unto their own
destruction.

Ye therefore beloved seeing ye know these things before, beware
lest ye also, being led away with the error of the wicked fall from your
own stedfastness. But grow in grace and in the knowledge of our
Lord and Savior Jesus Christ. To him be glory both now and forever
Amen. But as truly as I live all the earth shall be filled with the glory
of the Lord Thou shalt fear the Lord thy God and serve him and shalt
swear by his name. Ye shall not go after other God's, of the people
which are round about you." "For the Lord thy God is a jealous God
among you lest the anger of the Lord thy God be kindled against
thee, and destroy thee from off the face of the earth. Only with thine
eyes shalt thus behold and see the reward of the wicked. Because
thou hast made the Lord which is my refuse even the most high thy
habitation. There shall be no evil befall thee neither shall any plague
come high thy dwelling. For he shall give his angels charge over thee
to keep thee in all thy ways. Because he hath set his love upon me,
therefore will I deliver him I will set him on high, because he hath
known my name. He shall call upon me and I will answer him. I will
be with him in trouble. I will deliver him and honor him. With long
life will I satisfy him, and show him salvation. Holding fast the fruit-
ful word as he hath been taught that he may be able by sound doctrine both to exhort and to convince the gainsayer."

"Unto the pure all things are pure, but unto them that are defiled
and unbelieving is nothing pure, but even their mind and conscience
is defiled. They profess that they know God but in works they deny

him being abominable and disobedient and unto every good work reprobate. But speak thou the things which become sound doctrine. That the aged men be sober, grave, temperate, and sound in faith, in charity, in patience. The aged women likewise that they be in behavior as becomes holiness, not false accusers, not given too much wine, teachers of good things. That they may teach the young women to be sober to love their husbands, to love their children. To be discreet chaste keepers at home, good, obedient to their husbands, that the word of God be not blasphemed. Young men likewise exhort to be sober minded."

"In all things she wing thyself a pattern of good works in doctrine showing incorruptness, gravity, sincerity, sound, speech, that cannot be condemned, that he that is of the contrary part may be ashamed, having no evil thing to say of you. Exhort servants to be obedient unto their own masters and to please them well in all things, not answering again. Not purloining, but showing all good fidelity, that they may adorn the doctrine of God our savior in all things. For the grace of God that bringeth salvation hath appeared to all men. Teaching ungodliness and worldly lists, we should live soberly righteously, and sadly in this present world.

"Looking for that blessed hope, and the glorious appearing of the great God and our Savior Jesus Christ. Who gave himself for us that he might redeem us from all indignity, and purify unto himself a peculiar people, zealous of good works. These things speak, and exhort, and rebuke with all authority, let no man despise thee. To speak evil of no man, to be no brawlers but gentle she wing all meekness unto all men."

"For we ourselves also were sometimes foolish, disobedient, deceiving, serving diverse lusts and pleasures, living in malice and envy, hateful and hating one another. But after that the kindness and love of God our Savior toward man appeared. Not by works of righteousness which we have done, but according to his mercy he saved us, by the washing of regeneration and renewing of the Holy Ghost which he shed on us abundantly through Jesus Christ our Savior. That being justified by his grace, we should be made heirs according to the hope of eternal life.

"These things are good and profitable unto men. But avoid foolish questions and genealogies, and contentions, and strivings about the law, for they are unprofitable and vain. All that are with me salute thee. Greet them that love us in the faith. Grace be with you all. Amen."

"Neither let us commit fornication, as some of them committed and fell in one day three 6 twenty thousand. Neither let us tempt Christ as some of them also tempted and were destroyed of serpents. Neither murmur ye, as some of them also murmured and were destroyed of the destroyer. Now all these things happened unto them for ensamples Barbara Brown and they are written for our admonition, upon whom the ends of the world are come. Wherefore let him that thinketh he standeth take heed lest be fall. There hath no temptation taken you but such as is common to man. But God is faithful who will not suffer you to be tempted above that ye are able but will the temptation also make a way to escape, that ye may be able to bear it. Wherefore, my dearly beloved flee from idolatry. But I would have you know, that the head of every man is Christ, and the head of the woman is the man, and the head of Christ is God."

"This I say then, walk in the spirit, and ye shall not fulfill the flesh. For the flesh lusteth against the spirit, and the spirit against the flesh, and these are contrary the one to the other, so that ye cannot do the things that ye would. But if ye be led off the spirit, ye are not under the law.

For every man shall bear his own burden. Let him that is taught in the word communicate unto him that teacheth in all good things. Be not deceived, God is not mocked, for whatsoever a man soweth that shall he also reap. For he that soweth to his flesh shall of the flesh reap corruption but he that soweth to the spirit shall of the spirit reap life everlasting. And let us not be weary in well doing for in due seasons we shall reap if we faint not. As we have therefore

opportunity, let us do good unto all men, especially unto them who
are of the household of faith. Brethren, the grace of our Lord Jesus
Christ be with your spirit, Amen."

"But to which of the angels said he at anytime, sit on my right
hand, until I make thine thy footstool: For unto the angels hath he
not put in subjection the world to come, whereof we speak. Thou
made him a little lower than the angels, thou crownedst him with
glory and honor, and didst set him over the works of thy hands. Thou
last put all things in subjection under his feet. For in that he put all
in subjection under him, he left nothing that is not put under him,
but now we see not yet all things put under a little lower him, but we
see Jesus who was made a little lower than the angels for the suffering of death, crowned with glory and honor, that he by the grace of
God should taste death for every man. For it became him, for whom
are all things, and by whom are all things, in bringing many sons
unto glory, to make the captain of their salvation perfect through suf-
ferings. For both he that sanctified and they who are sanctified are
all of one, for which cause he is not ashamed to call them brethren
saying, I will declare thy name unto my brethren in the midst of the
church will I sing praise unto thee. And again, I will put my trust in
him. And again, Behold I and the children which God hath given me.
For as much then as the children are partakers of flesh and blood,
he also himself likewise took part of the same that through death he
might destroy him that had to power of death, that is the devil. And
deliver them who through fear of death were all their lifetime subject
to bondage. For verily he took not on him the nature of angels, but he
took on him the seed of Abraham. Wherefore in all things it beloved
him to be made like unto his brethren, that he might be merciful
Barbara Brown and things faithful high priest in things pertaining to
God. Now the works of the flesh are manifest, which are these, adultery, fornication, uncleanness, lasciviousness. Idolatry, witchcraft, ha-
tred, variance, emulation, wrath, strife, sedations heresies. Envyings,
murders, drunkenness, revellings, and such like of the which I tell
you before, as I have also told you in time past, that they which do

such things shall not inherit the kingdom of God. But the fruit of the spirit is love, joy, peace, longsuffering, gentleness, goodness, faith, meekness, temperance against such there is no law.

And they that are Christ's have crucified the flesh with the affections and lusts. If we live in the spirit, let us also walk in the spirit. Let us not be desirous of vain glory, provoking one another, envying one another."

"Brethren, If a man be overtaken in a fault, ye which are spiritual, restore such as one in the spirit of meekness, considering thyself, lest they also be tempted. Bear ye one another's burdens, and so fulfill the law of Christ. For if a man think himself to be something, when he is nothing, he deceiveth himself. But let every man prove his own work, and then shall he have rejoicing in another. Barbara Brown in himself alone and not in another to make reconciliation for the sins of the people. For in that he himself hath suffered being tempted his able to succor them that are tempted. WHEREFORE HOLY brethren partakers of the heavenly calling, consider the Apostle and High priest of our profession Christ Jesus.

"Harden not your hearts, as in the provocation in the day of temptation in the wilderness. when your fathers tempted me, proved me and saw my works forty years wherefore I was grieved with that generation, and said, they do always err in their heart, and they have not known my ways. So I share in my wrath they shall not enter into my rest. Take heed brethren, lest there be in any of you an evil heart of unbelief, in departing from the living God. But exhort one another daily, while it is called today lest any of you be hardened through the deceitfulness of sin. For we are made partakers of Christ, if we hold the beginning of our confidence steadfast unto the end while it is said today if ye will hear his voice, harden not your hearts, as in the provocation. And to whom swore he that they should not enter into his rest, but to them that he believed not? So we see that they could not enter in because of unbelief. Let us therefore fear Barbara Brown lest a promise being left us of eternity into his rest any of you should seem to come short of it.

For unto us was the gospel preached, as well as unto them, but the word preached did not profit them not being mixed with faith in them that heard it. For me which have believed do not enter into rest as he said, as I have sworn in my wrath, if the shall enter into my rest although the works were finished of the world. For he spoke in a certain place of the seventh day on this wise. And God did rest the seventh day from all his works. And in this place again, If they shall enter into my rest. Seeing therefore it remaineth that some must enter therein, and they to whom it was first preached entered not in because of unbelief. For if Jesus had given them rest, then would be not afterward have spoken of another day. There remaineth therefore a rest to the people of God. For he that is entered into his rest, he also hath ceased from his own works, as God did from his. Let us labor therefore to enter into that rest, lest any man fall after the same example of unbelief. For the word of God is quick and powerful, and sharper than any two edged sword piercing even to the dividing asunder of souls. Barbara Brown and spirit, and of the joints and marrow and is a discerner of the thoughts and intents of the heart.

"Neither is there any creature that is not manifest in his sight, but all things are naked and opened unto the eyes of him with whom we have to do. Seeing then that we have a great high priest, that is passed into the heavens, Jesus the son of God, let us hold fast our profession. For we have not an high priest which cannot be touched with the feeling of our infirmities, but was in all points tempted like as we are yet without sin. Let us therefore come badly into the throne of grace, that we may obtain mercy, and find grace to help in time of need."

"So also Christ glorified not himself to be made an high priest, but he that said unto him. Thou art my son, today have I begotten thee. Who in the days of his flesh when he had offered up prayer and supplications with strong crying and tears unto him that was able to save him from death, and was heard in the he feared. Though he were a son, yet learned he obedience by the things which he suffered. And being made perfect he became the author of eternal salvation unto all them that obey him. Called of God an high priest after the order of Melchizedek Barbara Brown. For when the time ye ought to be teachers, ye have need that one teach you again which be the first principle of the oracles of God and are become such as have need of milk, and not of strong meat. For everyone that useth milk is unskillful in the word of righteousness for he is a babe. But strong meat belongeth to them that are of full age, even those who by reason of use have their senses exercised to discern both good and evil. "THEREFORE LEAVING the principles of the doctrine of Christ, let us go on unto perfection, not laying again the foundation of repentance from deed works and of faith towards God of the doctrine of baptisms, and of laying on of hands, and of resurrection of the dead, and of eternal judgment. And this will we do, if God permit. For it is impossible for those who were once enlightened, and have tasted of the heavenly gift, and were made partakers of the Holy Ghost. And have tasted the good word of God, and the powers of the world to come. If they shall fall away, to renew them again unto repentance seeing they crucify to themselves the son of God afresh and put them in an open shame. For God is not unrighteousness to forget your work and labour of love, which ye have shewed toward his name in that ye have ministered to the saints, and do minister. And we desire the everyone of you do show the same diligence to the full assurance of hope unto the end. That we be not slothful but followers of them who through faith and patience inherit the promises.

"For such an high priest became us, who is holy, harmless, undefiled, separate from sinners, and made higher than the heavens. NOW OF the things which we have spoken this is the sum: We have such as high priest, who is set on the right hand of the throne of the Majesty in the heavens. But this man, after he had offered on sacrifice for sins forever, sat down on the right hand of God. From henceforth expecting till his enemies be made his footstool. For by on offering be hath perfected for ever them that are sanctified. Whereof the Holy Ghost also is a witness to us for after that he had said before. This is the covenant that I will make that I will make them after those days saith the Lord, I will put my laws into their hearts, and in their

minds will I write them. And their sins and iniquities will I remember
no more. Now where remission of these is, there is no more offering
for sin. Having therefore, brethren boldness to enter into the holiest
by the blood of Jesus. By a new and living way which he hath con-
secrated for us, through the veil, that is to his flesh. And having an
high priest over the house of God. Let us draw near with a true heart
in full assurance of faith, having our hearts sprinkled from an evil
conscience, and our bodies washed with pure water. Let us hold fast
the professions of our faith without wavering, for he is faithful that
promised. And let us consider one another to provoke unto love and
to good works. Now forsaking the assembling of ourselves together,
as the manner of some is, but exhorting one another and so much
the more, as ye see the day approaching. For if we sin willfully after
that we have received the knowledge of the truth, there remaineth
no more sacrifice for sins. For we know him that hath said, vengeance
belongeth unto me, I will recompense, saith the Lord. And again,
the Lord shall judge the people. It is a fearful thing to fall into the
hands of the living God. For ye have need of patience, that after ye
have done the will of God, ye might receive the promise. For yet a
little while, and he that shall come will come and will not tarry. Now
the just shall live by faith, but if any man drawback, my soul shall
have no pleasure in him. But we are not of them who draw back unto
perdition, but of them that believe to the saving of the soul. No faith
is the substance of things hoped for, the evidence of things not seen.
Through faith we understand that the worlds were framed by the
word of God, so that things which are seen were not made of things
which do appear. Amen.

But without faith it is impossible to please him for he that cometh
to God must believe that he is, and that he is a rewarder of them that
diligently seek him.

Follow peace with all men, and holiness without which no man
shall see the Lord. Let brotherly love continue. Be not forgetful to en-
tertain strangers, for thereby some have entertained angles unawares.
Remember them that are in bonds, as bound with them, and them

which suffer adversity, as being yourself also in the body. Marriage is honorable in all, and the bed undefiled, but whoremongers and adulterers God will judge. Let your conservation be without covetousness and be content with such things as ye have, for he hath said, I will never leave thee, nor forsake thee, so we may badly say. The Lord is my helper and I will not fear what man shall do unto me. Remember them which have rule over you, who have spoken unto you the word of God, whose faith follow considering the end of their conversation. Jesus Christ the same yesterday and today, and forever. By him therefore let us offer the sacrifice of praise to God continually, that is, the fruit of our lips giving thanks to his name. But to do good and to communicate forget not, for with sacrifices God is well pleased. Obey them that have the rule over you and submit yourselves for they watch for your souls, as they that must give account, that they may do it with joy, and not with grief for that is unprofitable for you. Pray for us we trust we have a good conscience, in all things willing to live honesty. Now the God of peace that brought again from the dead our Lord Jesus, that great shepherd of the sheep, through the blood of the everlasting covenant. Make you perfect in every good works to do his will working in you that which is well pleasing in his sight, through Jesus Christ to whom be glory forever and ever Amen."

"My brethren count it all joy when ye fall into divers temptation. Knowing this that the trying of your faith worketh patience. But let patience have her perfect work, that ye may be perfect and entire wanting nothing. If any of you lack wisdom let him ask of God, that giveth to all men liberally, and upbraideth not, and unbraideth not, and it shall be given him. But let him ask in faith nothing wavering. For he that waver this like a wave of the sea driven with the wind and tossed. For let not that man think that he shall receive anything of the Lord. A double minded man is unstable in all ways." "Let the brother of low degree rejoice that he is exalted. But the rich, in that he is made low, because as the flower of the grass he shall pass away. For the sun is no sooner risen with a burning heat, but it withereth the grass, and the flower thereof falleth, and the grace of the fashion of it perisheth, so shall the rich man fade away in his ways." "Blessed is the man that endureth temptation for when he is tried, he shall receive the crown of life, which the Lord hath promised to them that love him. Let no man say when he is tempted, I am tempted of God, for God cannot be tempted with evil, neither tempteth he any man. But every man is tempted, when he is drawn away of his own lust, and enticed. Then when lust has conceived, it brigeth forth sin and sin is death, when it is finished bringeth forth death. Every good gift and every perfect gift is from above and cometh down from the father of lights, with whom is no variableness neither shadow of turning. Of his own will begat he us with the word of truth, that we should be a kind of first fruits of his creatures. Wherefore my beloved brethren, let every man be swift to hear, slow to speak, slow to wrath. Wherefore lay apart all filthiness and superfluity of naughtiness, and receive with meekness the engrafted word which is able to save your souls. But be ye doers of the word, and of hears only deceiving your own selves. For if any be a hearer of the word, and not a doer, he is like unto a man beholding his natural face in a glass. For he be holdeth himself and goeth his way, and straightway forgetteth what manner of man he was. But whoso looketh into the perfect law of liberty, and continueth therein he being not a forgetful hearer, but a doer of the work, this man shall be blessed in his deed. If any man among you seem to be religious, and bridleth not his tongue, but deceiveth his own heart, this man's religion is vain. Pure religion and undefiled before God and the father is this. To visit the fatherless and widows in their affliction and to keep himself unspotted from the world. Hearken my beloved brethren. Hath not God chosen the poor of his world rich in faith, and heirs of the kingdom which he hath promised to them that love him. If ye fulfil the royal law according to the scripture thou shalt love thy neighbor as thyself ye do well. For whosoever shall keep the whole law, and yet offend in one point, he is guilty of all. For he that said, do not commit adultery, said also, do not kill. Now if thou commit no adultery said also, do not kill. Now if thou commit no adultery, yet if thou kill thou art become a transgressor of the law.

What doeth it profit, my brethren, though a man say he hath faith, and have not works? Can faith save him. Even so faith, if it hath not works is dead being alone. Yea, a man may say thou last faith, and I have works, show me thy faith without thy works, and I will show thee my faith by my works. Thou believest that there is one God thou does't well the devil also believe and tremble. For as the body without the spirit is dead, so faith without works is dead. Even so the tongue is a little member, and boasteth great things, behold, how great a matter a little fire kindleth! And the tongue is a fire a world of iniquity, so is the tongue among our members that it defileth the whole body and setteth on fire the course of nature, any it is set on fire of hell. For every kind of breasts and of birds, and of serpents and of things in the sea, is tamed and hath been tamed of mankind. But the tongue can no man tame it is unruly evil, full of deadly poison. Out of the same mouth proceedeth blessing, and cursing. My brethren these things ought not so to be. Who is a wise man and endued with knowledge among you? Let him show out of a good conversation his works with weakness of wisdom.

"Be patient therefore brethren unto the coming of the Lord, Behold the husband man waith for the precious fruit of the earth, and hath long patience for it, until he received the early and latter rain. Be ye also patient stablish your hearts, for the coming of the Lord draweth high. Grudge not one against another brethren, lest ye be condemned, behold, the judge standeth before the door. Behold we count them happy which endure. You have heard of the patience of job and have seen the end of the Lord is very pitiful, and of tender mercy. But above all things my brethren, swear not, neither by heaven, neither by the earth, neither by any other oath, but let your yea be yea, and your hay, hay, lest ye fall into condemnation." "Is any among you afflicted? Let him pray, Is any merry, Let him sing psalms, Is any sick among you let him call for the elders of the church, and the pray over him. Anointing him with oil in the name of the Lord. And the prayer of faith shall save the sick, and the Lord shall raise him up and if he hath committed sins, they shall be forgiven him.

Confess your faults one to another, and pray one for another that
we may be healed. The effectual fervent prayer of a righteous man
availeth much. Let him know, that he which converteth the sinner
from the error of his way shall save a soul from death, and shall hide
a multitude of sins.

"Remembering without ceasing your work of faith, and labor of
love, and patience of hope in our Lord Jesus Christ, in the sight of
God and our Father. Knowing brethren beloved, your election of God.
For our gospel came not unto you in word only, but also in power, and
in the Holy Ghost, and in much assurance as ye know what manner
of men we were among you for your sake. And ye became followers of
us and of the Lord, having received the word in much affliction, with
joy of the Holy Ghost. As ye know how we exhorted and comforted
and charged everyone of you, as a father doth his children. For this
cause also thank we God without ceasing, because when ye received
the word of God which ye heard of us, ye received is not as the word
of men, but as it is in truth, the word of God, which effectually worketh also in you that believe. For what is our hope, or joy, or crown of
rejoicing? Are not even ye in the presence of our Lord Jesus Christ
at his coming? For now we live, if ye stand fast in the Lord for what
thanks can we render to God again for you for all the joy.

Where with we joy for your sakes before our God night and day
praying exceedingly that we might see your face, and might perfect
that which is lacking in your faith? Now God himself and our Father,
and our Lord Jesus Christ, direct our way unto you. And the Lord
make you to increase and abound in love one toward another, and
toward all men even as we do toward you. To the end he may stablish
your hearts unblameable in holiness before God, even our Father, at
the coming of our Lord Jesus Christ with all saints. FURTHERMORE
then we beseech you, brethren and exhort you by the Lord Jesus, that
as ye ought to walk and to please God, so ye would abound more and
more, For ye know what commandments we gave you by the Lord
Jesus. For this is the will of God, even your sanctification, that ye
should abstain from fornication that everyone of you should know

how to possess his vessel in sanctification and honour. Not in the lust of concupiscence, even as the gentiles which know not God. That no man go beyond and defraud his brother in any matter, because that the Lord in the avenger of all such, as we also have forewarned you and testified. For God hath not called us to uncleanness, but into holiness. He therefore that despiseth despiseth not man, but God, who hath also given unto us his holy spirit. That ye may walk honestly toward them that are without, and that ye may have lack of nothing. But I would not have you to be ignorant, brethren, concerning them which are asleep, that ye sorrow not even as others which have no hope. For if we believe that Jesus died and rose again, even so them also which sleep in Jesus will God bring with him. For this we say unto you by the word of the Lord, that we which are alive and remain unto the coming of the Lord shall not prevent them which are asleep. For the Lord himself shall descend from heaven with a shout, with the voice of the archangel and with the trump of God and the dead on Christ shall raise first. Then we which are alive and remain shall be caught up together with them in the clouds, to meet the Lord in the air and so shall we ever be with the Lord wherefore comfort one another with these words. For yourselves know perfectly that the day of the Lord, so cometh as a thief in the night. But ye, brethren are not as a thief in the night. But ye, brethren are not in darkness, that day should overtake you as a thief, ye are all the children of light, and the children of the day: We are not of the night nor of darkness. Therefore let us not sleep as do others, but let us watch and be sober. For they that sleep, sleep in the night, and they that be drunken are drunken in the night. But let us, who are of the day, be sober, putting on the breastplate of faith and love and for an helmet, the hope of salvation. For God hath not appointed us to wrath, but to obtain salvation by our Lord Jesus Christ. Who died for us, that whether we wake or sleep, we should live together for him. Wherefore comfort yourselves together, and edify one another even as also ye do. Now we exhort you brethren, warn them that are unruly, comfort the feeble-minded support the weak, be patient toward all men. See that none render evil for evil unto any man, but ever follow that which is good, both among yourselves and to all men rejoice evermore pray without ceasing. In everything give thanks for this is the will of Jesus Christ Jesus concerning you. Quench not the spirit. Despise not prophesyings. Prove all things hold fast that which is good. Abstain all appearance of evil. And the very God of peace sanctify you wholly and I pray God your whole spirit and soul and body be preserved blameless unto the coming of our Lord Jesus Christ. Faithful is he that calleth you, who also will do it. Greet all the brethren with an holy kiss. The grace of our Lord Jesus Christ be with you. Amen.

# CONCLUSION

### <u>Song of Praise</u>

Sometimes during our journey there will be ups and downs. Some people will be with you during the good times and not with you during the bad. It can go either way. Don't expect people to always support you during your joy. Remember it is only through your relationship between you and God. Never let anyone take away your joy enjoy your moment. Some people have a negative spirit. They have not fully come into the understanding of their calling of God. When we meet up with God and he allowed us to see the rewards of our journey, then we can lift up our voice and praise him for how he brought us through.

TO GOD BE THE GLORY FOR THE THINGS HE HAS DONE. AMEN.

Peace and Love,
Barbara Brown

9 780692 685341